To: Chris

# 3G Connection

## GO TO GOD
## GROW WITH GRACE
## GLOW IN GLORY

May GOD richly bless you!

# NATASHA JUGGER

*Natasha Jugger*

**3G Connection: Go to God, Grow with Grace, Glow in Glory**

All rights reserved. Published in the United States by Pipe Publishing, a division of the Stimuknowlogy Institute LLC Fort Pierce, Florida.

www.writeabookin31days.com

Biblical references from New King James Version (NKJV); New International Version (NIV), King James Version (KJV); and The Message (MSG)

3G Connection may be purchased in bulk for educational or promotional use. For information please contact **www.3GConnection.com**

Library of Congress Cataloging-In-Publication Data
Jugger, Natasha

3G connection: go to god, grow with grace, glow in glory/Natasha Jugger

First Edition.

ISBN 978-0-692-05019-4

1. Religious Warfare    2. Religions & Inspirations

Library of Congress Control Number: 2018931944

Cover and interior design by Stacey Grainger

Printed in the United States of America
First Edition

"To You, O God of my fathers, I give thanks and praise, For You have given me wisdom and power; Even now You have made known to me what we requested of You, For You have made known to us the king's matter."

**– Daniel 2:23**

Through the Word of God, we are granted wisdom. Through the Holy Spirit, we can access the power of Our Father, God. To experience more love, wisdom, and power in your life, Visit me at
**www.3GConnection.com**
and pick up your complimentary copy of
*The A, B, C's of a Joyful Life.*

*To inspired Christians who are dedicated
to the expansion of God's Kingdom*

# Contents

# A Mother's Thoughts

Part of my life's legacy has been fulfilled in the writing of this book. As a mother raising a millennial daughter, I have experienced both rewards and challenges. She doesn't even know the nights I stayed awake when I heard, "I'm going to the club, mama." I cried. "Lord, where did I go wrong?" I thought I was this single mom raising a child in the Spirit of God, and in His grace and glory. But weeping endures for a night, my spirit would soon leap for joy at the day when she called me on the phone and said, "Mama, the Holy Ghost would have me to tell you this…" Everything I instilled in her from birth was now coming full circle and it was a beautiful sight to behold.

If we have a generation that doesn't know how to go to God, and understand that He can take them from where they are or have been, to a place in His glory, then we raise a nation of people deprived of a genuine connection to God's grace and glory. To wallow in a lifestyle of unrighteousness is to dwell in a place void of life and potentiality. An understanding of God's love and promise of restoration involves a process. It is a process of knowing that we have a God who cares about us so much so, that He allows us to go through the toils of discovery.

I am honored to be have been acquainted with my daughter's process of experiencing God's love. His Word truly does not return void.

"Train up a child in the way he should go:
and when he is old, he will not depart from it."

She now walks in the way of righteousness and holiness. What a legacy? The beauty in watching the process of her Go and Grow, is that Glory will be passed to her offspring. Generational curses will be broken and blessings will abound. There is humility in seeing my daughter mature in Christ. This is the glory of God. I dare not say it is me. I did not give her an oratorical gift...that eloquence, passion, and purpose will enable her to speak to and pray for a generation that needs spiritual intercession.

Thank you, Holy Spirit, for establishing my purpose and allowing me and my child to confidently Go, Grow, and Glow in order to obtain the Gift of eternal life.

*Pharis Ebanks*

Mother, Friend, Sister in Christ
Author of *Know What Brings Laughter to His Ears*

# Introduction

I magine a life filled with endless possibilities of success. Not to say there will not be trials and tribulations, but visualize a way out every time your back is up against the wall. Christ never promised a life free of hardships, but He promised peace (John 16:33).

This book is about engaging in radical self-confrontation. Reflect on the statements and questions posed at the end of every section. Allow God to deal with your innermost thoughts and true heart posture towards His will. As you progress through this book, God will transform your mind and renew your heart. You will have a new outlook on life - one that encourages you to overcome fears and propels you further into your destiny.

The essence of a 3G connection is God, the grace He gives us, and the glory that shines through for the grace we wear. Without a 3G connection, life is absent of God, Grace, and Glory. It is a life filled with restlessness, brokenness, and damage. It's a life not well lived. A life not well spent. It's a life not worth living.

Missing the 3G connection, I whirled in a bondage of sin. This left even bigger gaps of brokenness and bitterness. But, God delivered me from a life of void. Despite all I have experienced, God is faithful, just, and willing to forgive and purify me (1 John 1:9). He gives us free will. It is our choice to be obedient. There is freedom and reward in obedience. The freedom to worship God in spirit and in truth is something we take for granted. Worship brings about restoration; there is nothing like the presence of the Lord.

It's important for me to live the life I live now; not perfect, but upright and righteous. Examples stand before me in the Word of God. A blessed life allows me to testify about His grace and goodness. I am positioned to draw others to Christ as someone once did for me.

Have you ever met someone who could not 'catch a break' or experienced little good in their life? Those are the people I desire to reach. I was once in the same place and know what it takes to get untangled. The answer is to Go to God, Grow with Grace, and Glow in Glory.

# 3G Connection with 4G Connectivity

Merriam-Webster defines connection as, "the placing or establishing of a relationship." Connectivity is defined as, "the state or quality of being connected." When you establish a relationship with Christ, you connect to God in three ways; God the Father, God the Son, and God the Holy Spirit. The 3G connection with Christ provides a 4G connectivity with a God who remains connected, despite our uncertainty and persuasions. You, me, no one can outdo God's demonstration of love. He gives us connectivity to eternal life, even when 3G connection is static.

Go, Grow, and Glow make up the 3G connection framework. The 4Gs are God, Grace, Glory, and the Gift of Eternal Life. Go is defined as, "habitually being in a certain state or condition." To grow is "to spring up and develop into maturity." A glow is, "a steady radiance of light." As God presented it to me, if you do not go, then you can't grow. If you don't grow, you won't glow. Growing without going keeps you in the same place. You risk stagnation for years and stunt your growth. Glowing without growing reflects self-help, not Gods' help. This results in limited success. However, glowing with glory equates to infinite blessings. The world's view of success is short lived. Blessings are lifelong. God wants to bless your success, and He wants you to live in eternity.

# The Go, Grow, and Glow Process

Do as God instruct you to do. Grow and prosper as you follow His instructions. Glow increasingly each day as your obedience increases. Those inside the will of God exude a certain glow. If you go to God, He will do His part. And God will do more on your behalf than you will do. Go to Him in spirit and in truth. He turns messes into beauty. That is the first gift towards eternal life.

Next, you must grow. It is impossible to mature into the things of God and remain dormant. Dormancy stagnates and will not only cloud your destiny, but shade blessings for others who depend on your growth. Communication with God is intentional dialogue between you and Christ. It requires you speak, then listen for His reply. It is not enough to speak to God and not wait on His reply. The point of communication is to receive His impartations and grow with them as they grow with you. Impartations are not meant for you to keep to yourself, but rather for you to live out. Daily living out God's impartations based on His Holy Word allows you to grow. Impartations without growth makes room for silence. God stops speaking when He senses you're no longer listening. Listening implies attunement of your voice to His ears, then application to your life. Growth only comes from doing. God rewards the hearers and doers of His Holy Word (Matthew 7:24).

Maturity is not emotion based. Maturity says, "God, what do you want me to do?" That is how you grow. That is growing with grace. Growth requires grace because sometimes God stretches us. He pulls us, and He makes us into a new creation. Often what He asks us to do may seem uncomfortable. Grace enters here. God says, "Okay, I asked you to do this. Now, I will extend you grace to do it." You grow with grace as His grace on your life grows. If you fail, if you fall, if you stumble, His grace is sufficient. His grace is enough to keep you through it all.

To glow in glory is the final phase in the 3G Connection process. I do not look like what I have been through. I do not even look like the people I hung around in sin. The new me is a part of the glow that God gives. God does not want you to look like what you have been through. He doesn't want you to look a mess or behave like a mess. God wants you to glow. He wants the world to see your triumph, courage, and confidence. Your glow should make it almost impossible for others to fathom the sinful life you lived before your encounter with God. That is the glow He wants for you and for me.

Glow brings an outward appearance that is first reflected on the inside. It is an attraction to your anointing. Your glow is an anointing and people see something special. This is key to who you attract, and the energy you emit. God desires for us to look like who He has called us to be, not who we were outside His will. When I first came to know who I was in Christ, I had a hard time changing my attire to less revealing of skin. I conversed with God about my struggle. "God, why can't I wear what I want?" His response was simple. "I want you to look like who I've called you to be." Today, I realize I can dress appropriately and be beautiful. I am covered (in clothing) and covered (in Christ). My glow is appropriate, attractive, and anointed.

## Concerning the 4G Connectivity

If you go, grow, and glow, you will receive the gift of eternal life through God, His grace, and His glory. All things work together for the good of those who love Him and are called according to His purpose (Romans 8:28). The gift of eternal life is from God alone. God's grace is all over your life. Every day is an opportunity to do what He commands. This does not mean you won't go through hardships. The promise of eternal life is your gift. That's better than anything you can ever imagine. It is His grace. You can't get the gift of eternal life if you don't have blessings of His grace.

Without God, there is no grace. Without grace, there is no glory. A glorious life represents a life abundant with connections. The Holy Spirit revealed that eternal life is not just for me. Eternal life is for my children's children and for generations to come. While I may dwell in heaven, my legacy is eternal. It is the same for you and your offspring. What an awesome inheritance for your children? His glory should shine through the eternal life of your generation, your children's generation, and your ascension to heaven.

# Deborah's **4G Connectivity**

Deborah's life is a good illustration of the 4G Connectivity. She was a Biblical woman of God, judge, prophetess, warrior, wife, and mother. Some may see her roles as overwhelming. However, 3G connection (Go, Grow, and Glory) allowed her to demonstrate 4G connectivity in prophesies. She held 4G connectivity in battle, in marriage, and 4G connectivity with those who sought her. Deborah went to God. She grew, and she glowed. Because of the strength of the connection with God, she walked in a spirit of excellence. To hear from God, she first had to go to Him. You, like Deborah, must spend time in God's presence. Deborah laid out decrees and spoke to

Barak with boldness and confidence. This was a show of the time she spent in God's presence. Boldness results from embracing God's sovereignty and power. Deborah consulted God in all areas of her life. The way you speak, the way you walk, and the way you carry yourself shows if you are going to God for counsel. Others will know when you are not consulting the Holy Spirit. Actions are resounding.

The Bible tells us Barak was afraid to go into battle. His fears pushed Deborah into a place of maturity and growth. Her response, "I'll go with you." Leaders lead leaders. You must do what you have instructed others to do. If not, you risk effectiveness as a leader. Deborah exemplified bold leadership. Her explanation to Barak showed grace. She did not use insults or call him a cowardly man. She extended grace in her response. Sensing his fear, she said to Barak, "I'll go with you, but because of the course you are taking, you will not get all the honor." That is a gracious way to say, "You're acting like a coward." At the end of the battle, Deborah received glory because she did as God instructed. God will give you the correct way to respond to all situations in life, but you must be in a position to hear His voice. Positioned, you lead by the Holy Spirit, not emotions. This requires growth and maturity.

Glowing in glory, people came from many parts of the country to visit Deborah as she sat under the tree of Ephraim. They sought her for wise counsel. Like Deborah, your glow shines before you say anything. Your lifestyle speaks for itself. It should scream, "I love God and I love God's people!" Connecting with God's people and sharing His Word is part of the 3G Connection. Deborah acknowledged God and received both glory and honor.

My purpose in this book is to move people of God to follow a process for a more fulfilled life. The process includes going to God. He will help you grow and mature to attain His grace. Growth results in an outward glow that attracts others to your anointing and to His glory.

# GO TO GOD

Verse 1 – 8 of Judges Chapter 4 deals with the results of Going to God, or lack thereof. In verse 1, the Israelites' trust in Ehud rather than trust in God, the people saw no need to go to God. They suffered great consequences because of their choice. The Israelites face consequences of misguided reverence and lack of respect (verse 2). The Word reveals what happens when we tire of trying to do things on our own (verse 3). The rewards of going to God is demonstrated in verse 4. Quality time spent with Him can result in a prosperous life. As their judge, Deborah lead others to seek the wisdom of God (verse 5). In verse 6, God gives authority to give His commands to His people. He trusts Doers of His Word to deliver messages correctly and on time. God gives divine strategies to get through the battles at hand (verse 7). In verse 8, not going to God results in a lack of confidence. We rely on others to relay messages from God, instead of hearing from Him directly. To give accurate instructions, Deborah connected to God intimately. Likewise, we must have a relationship with Him to hear and recognize His voice in a crowd of millions.

# Judges 4:1 (NIV)

"Again, the Israelites did evil in the eyes of the Lord, now that Ehud was dead."

We often backslide when we think no one is watching or no one cares. God always watches over us, and He always cares. He sees and knows all. He is waiting for us to get it together.

### *Again – to repeat over and over*

We know the answer to a question, yet still ask. We know how to get to where we need to be, yet we head in a different direction. We know because of experiences, yet we repeat history. Our purpose serves others as much as it serves us. If we get tripped up on the small things, we miss our purpose.

What will it take for us to do as commanded? Many times, it requires a wake-up call before we run to our heavenly Father. Drastic measures should not be necessary to grab our attention, but we often operate in the flesh. God will allow us to get entangled in our mess until there is seemingly no way out. It is often at the last minute we realize there is only one real way out; Jesus Christ. God does not do this to embarrass us or to make us fear Him. Instead, He does this to save us from further embarrassment. It allows us to appreciate and reverence Him even more. God is not a God of tyranny. Rather, He is a God of many chances.

Identify your 'it,' the thing that distracts you from purpose. How can you get it right with God today?

_____

_____

_____

_____

_____

_____

_____

_____

_____

_____

_____

_____

_____

_____

_____

_____

_____

## *Ehud – united*

Ehud, the judge, was called to govern and unite the Israelites. The people of Israel, however, feared Ehud's judgment more than they feared the wrath of God. If they truly reverenced God, they would have understood that God was the ultimate judge of their sins, not Ehud.

"When you judge His name, be careful the preacher ain't your God" (Franklin). Here, we are reminded not to hold pastors in higher esteem than God. God places church leaders in our lives as an earthly extension of Himself; they are not God. Holding a pastor or any man or woman of God, for that matter, to such a high esteem will only bring disappointment, resentment, and anger. When men or women of God fall from grace, we tend to get angry and rebel against God because we often wonder why such an amazing God would allow one of His children to fall. A man will transgress for even the smallest of reasons (Proverbs 28:21). This should be a reality check for us to make sure that we are following God's agenda and not our own. Do not get angry with God, nor the man or woman of God, but see failing as a humbling experience for them and us. We must diligently search for ways in us that may result in the same fate. Seek to glorify God, not man.

Why do you think some people fear man more than they fear God?

_____

_____

_____

_____

_____

_____

_____

_____

_____

_____

_____

_____

_____

_____

_____

_____

# Judges 4:2 (NIV)

---

"So, the Lord sold them into the hands of Jabin king of Canaan, who reigned in Hazor. Sisera, the commander of his army, was based in Harosheth Haggoyim."

---

After some time, the Lord will give you over to sinful ways. You will experience a life far worse than anything you could ever imagine.

### The Lord sold them

Whatever you use against God, become the things God will use to get your attention. You may want to be in control all the time, and, in a relationship with someone who wants to control you. In this Bible story, the Israelites turned to pagan worship, fornication, and wickedness among many other things. They neglected God and did evil things in His sight. King Jabin then came to enslave them. He put them back in bondage and did wickedness unto them. Often, God will not step in your situation until you repent and turn to Him. God watched and waited for His people to acknowledge that He alone is God, and He alone could save them.

Today, if you are dealing with issues of pride, put your pride away and cry out to God. He will hear your cry, forgive your sins, and heal your land (2 Chronicles 7:14). Healing can take place in all aspects of life, including your finances, family, and faith.

Will God, give you over to a reprobate mind? Or, will you give yourself over to God before it is too late?

_____

_____

_____

_____

_____

_____

_____

_____

_____

_____

_____

_____

_____

_____

_____

_____

_____

## *Canaan – humility*

God has a way of humbling His people; He allowed the Israelites capture into slavery. Do not take credit for the good things that happen in your life and do not blame God for the bad. Many times, bad things are humbling experiences. Our Father said He will never leave, nor forsake you. He will see you through to deliverance.

We are all taken captive by different circumstances, but it is up to us to break free from the monotony of sin. It is hard to be humble if we cannot accept that God, our Father, just wants the best for us. Resistance to His will results in pride and disgrace (Proverbs 11:2). Pride is an all too familiar feeling for a lot of us. Pride will get you nowhere but stuck.

Will you be humbled by your experiences, or lose humility because of your experiences?

_____

_____

_____

_____

_____

_____

_____

_____

_____

_____

_____

_____

_____

_____

_____

_____

# Judges 4:3 (NIV)

---

"Because he had nine hundred chariots fitted with iron and had cruelly oppressed the Israelites for twenty years, they cried to the Lord for help."

---

Once we get sick and tired of being sick and tired, that is when we usually cry out to the Lord for deliverance from a situation. Too often, we do not run into His arms until something horrible happens.

## Nine – judgment

Throughout the Bible, the number nine represented judgment. Peter and John prayed at the ninth hour, an hour at which ungodly things may take place (Acts 3:1). There are nine fruits of the spirit in which to govern ourselves (Galatians 5:22-23). God reigned down His judgment upon the people of Israel, and there was nothing they could do but trust and believe in the power of God's Word. God will get you to a place of submission—a place where you must seek His face for forgiveness and direction. He will send judgment your way, but not without a plan. To test your strength in the face of adversity, God will put you to the test.

Whether it is one person or an entire congregation of people against you, will you believe what God says about you, or believe what man says about you?

_____

_____

_____

_____

_____

_____

_____

_____

_____

_____

_____

_____

_____

_____

_____

_____

_____

### *Twenty – completion of a divinely-ordered waiting period*

The number twenty represents completion throughout the Bible. For twenty years, Jacob worked to be free (Genesis 31:41). Samson judged Israel for twenty years before his time ended (Judges 15:20). After twenty years, the people of God rejected oppression and cried out unto God. It took twenty years for them to realize the detriment of their situation. Before it is too late, realize where you are, where you want to be, and how you plan to get there. Do not place limits on God. Twenty years is the time it took for the Israelites to be free. It is not necessarily the time it will take for you to be free of bondage in your life.

Time is an element we cannot retrieve. Identify areas in your life where a wiser use of time can be beneficial. What is your plan for better use of time?

_____

_____

_____

_____

_____

_____

_____

_____

_____

_____

_____

_____

_____

_____

_____

_____

# Judges 4:4 (NIV)

"Now Deborah, a prophet, the wife of Lappidoth,
was leading Israel at that time."

Deborah, a woman, redefined a nation for God. He does not care about your age, gender, or marital status. No matter the title you are assigned, He will use you to lead His people if you are willing. Willingness gives way to opened doors of opportunity.

### Deborah – bee

Just because God used a woman does not mean men are not needed in the Kingdom. A woman was used to fulfill a role in that season. Deborah is defined as a bee. She was a queen bee in the land she governed. Deborah was selfless, willing to sacrifice her life on behalf of other worker bees in the land. Her words may have stung and her judgments harsh, but she instructed the people in righteousness as God instructed her. At other times, the Word she delivered may have been soft, sweet, and encouraging. Whatever the situation, she said what God instructed, went where she was sent, and delivered His message so the people could receive deliverance. Through Deborah, God downloaded instructions, redefined a nation, and activated purpose so others could reach their destiny.

A Deborah does not have to be a woman. Deborah can be anyone who has authority to deliver the uncompromising Word of God, despite backlash and judgement.

Are you willing to receive instructions, corrections, and tough love from the Deborah God has placed in your life? Can you identify Deborah's around you? Do you hope to one day identify yourself as Deborah? Why or why not?

_____

_____

_____

_____

_____

_____

_____

_____

_____

_____

_____

_____

_____

_____

*Prophet – an individual who is chosen by God to be His mouthpiece and lead his people in truth*

There is nothing wrong with the title of prophet or prophetess when appointed by God. Before we are male or female, we are human and united with other Believers. God is no respecter of title, gender, age, or ethnicity and we should not be either.

We are not in the business of convenience. We are, however, in the business of saving souls no matter the inconvenience. When we get past insecurities, we will be free to call ourselves whatever God desires. There is no distinction in the Kingdom of God. We are all His children and should treat each other as such. Respect of persons is not good (Proverbs 28:21). If others refer to you as a prophet or prophetess, be sure you hear from God on how He wants you to operate.

God has no respecter of title. Are you willing to, or have you heard from God concerning your placement? Or, have you appointed yourself?

_____

_____

_____

_____

_____

_____

_____

_____

_____

_____

_____

_____

_____

_____

_____

_____

_____

## *Lappidoth – light*

Surround yourself with fellow citizens in the body of Christ who shed light on who you are called to be (Matthew 5:16). Lappidoth is significant because Deborah needed someone who could light up her life during dark times. He shed light on revelations she received from God. Although Lappidoth was a guide, she allowed the Holy Spirit to lead.

When there is a power outage in your house, you have two options:

1. You can get a flashlight.
2. You can wait for the power to power up again.

When you go out during the eye of the storm, rather than wait for the gale to cease, you risk exposure to the most dangerous part of the weather. We do the same with God. When there is calm in our lives, we do not realize a storm may brew on the other side of our decisions. We expend time and energy thinking about and justifying our actions rather than waiting on God. We grow impatient with His response or what we view as a lack of response rather than see the bigger picture and wait in silence. Wait a little longer. The light of God will soon reflect the reasons you were supposed to wait. You are in fact worth the wait.

Wait on the Lord and be of good courage (Psalms 27:14). Do not look for temporary fixes that leave you guessing and empty inside. There will be no peace, reassurance, or sunshine in relationships outside the will of God.

Are you willing to wait out the storm? Or, are you caught in the storms of life?

_____

_____

_____

_____

_____

_____

_____

_____

_____

_____

_____

_____

_____

_____

_____

_____

_____

_____

_____

# Judges 4:5 (NIV)

---

"She held court under the Palm of Deborah
between Ramah and, Bethel in the hill country
of Ephraim, and the Israelites went up to her
to have their disputes decided."

---

If there is a peaceful place on the inside of
you where God can dwell, nothing that comes
up against you will be too difficult to address.
God will give you wisdom on how to handle all
situations.

### *Palm of Deborah*

God wants to put us on display for the world
to see as evidence of His glory. Deborah
was exalted on the outskirts of the city; a
place where people could get to her if they
were willing. Her heart posture towards God
gave her the authority to judge righteously.
Wherever God places you, it is a testament to
your character and the character of those who
surround you and seek you. The same life of
opulence and excellence Deborah lived is the
same life God desires for us to live. God will
get the glory from our lives when we exalt His
name above our own. Deborah was easy to
reach, but still guarded.

Make yourself available to those who desire to know more about the Christ in you and the God you serve. Advise when needed, but never condemn. Yes, the wages of sin are death (Romans 6:23), but no sin is greater than another. Be willing to deliver the Word of the Lord concerning the life of others.

Are you prepared to be put on display? Or, do you need to be in hiding a little while longer?

_____

_____

_____

_____

_____

_____

_____

_____

_____

_____

_____

_____

_____

_____

## *Bethel – God's house; His holy place*

Deborah was elevated to a higher place in God, a holy and righteous place. A lot of us house God in our hearts temporarily. He becomes a weary traveler, only invited in when we need Him. We treat God as a temporary fix rather than a permanent solution. Our house would be so much cleaner if we would allow Him to stay forever.

No one knows the hour, or the day Jesus Christ will return, except God the Father (Mark 13:32). We should aspire to be like Deborah. Do not wait for the end to draw near, but allow Him to live within you today. A life without God is no life.

"He that dwelleth in the secret place of the most High shall abide under the shadow of the almighty" (Psalm 91:1). We are dwellers in His secret place. We must abide by the house rules God has established for us. Each of us dwells differently. It is up to you not to allow the way others dwell to affect how you function. When you enter the dwelling of others, be mindful of respect, but do not change who you are in Christ.

Will God dwell on the inside of you, or will He be on the outside looking in? How do you set your dwelling apart from the world?

_____

_____

_____

_____

_____

_____

_____

_____

_____

_____

_____

_____

_____

_____

_____

_____

_____

## *Disputes decided*

When others turn to you for advice, consult the Holy Spirit before you speak. If He permits you to speak, then speak. If He wants you to listen that is what you must do. God will give you wisdom when He says move. When He says do, you do. However, where God is silent, be still, wait, and know He is God (Psalm 46:10).

Will you speak out of turn or speak when instructed by God?

_____

_____

_____

_____

_____

_____

_____

_____

_____

_____

_____

_____

_____

_____

_____

_____

# Judges 4:6 (NIV)

---

"She sent for Barak son of Abinoam from Kedesh in Naphtali and said to him, "The Lord, the God of Israel, commands you: 'Go, take with you ten thousand men of Naphtali and Zebulun and lead them up to Mount Tabor.'"

---

God expects us to follow every command He gives to us. Do not worry about what it looks like on the outside or how many people you have in your corner. God is concerned with your lifelong pursuit of Him, not your shortcomings.

### She sent for Barak

In the Biblical days, it was not typical for a woman to send for a man. However, God uses whoever He needs to get our attention. When the call comes, it is up to us to answer. Like Barak, God will find you wherever you are. Do not think you can hide.

As a college student, I thought I was in the perfect place to hide from God. I was like many of my peers, passive about God, His commandments, and His promises. I recall a college friend who was repeatedly invited to church, but made excuses for not being able to attend. One Sunday, however, her mom visited her. She knew she had to get up and go to church because she had told her mom she attended services every week. The only place she could think to go was the place she had been frequently invited. The Sunday of her 'by chance' attendance to church, she accepted Christ as her personal Savior. Since that time, God has been working in her life. He is not done perfecting the work in her, but many are happy to see the progress she has made with Gods' help and help from people He placed in her life.

Just as Deborah gave Barack a little push, my friend needed a nudge to move from complacency. She is grateful for the ministry. To this day, she thanks God for divine intervention. There are no coincidences in the Kingdom.

Connect yourself with a ministry that allows you to grow. Growth comes through pushing further into the things of God. Do not get comfortable in ministry, or growth stunts. Uncomfortability promotes healthy growth and prosperity.

When you are called to minister, how will you respond?

_____

_____

_____

_____

_____

_____

_____

_____

_____

_____

_____

_____

_____

_____

_____

_____

_____

# Judges 4:7 (NIV)

---

"I will lead Sisera, the commander of Jabin's army, with his chariots and his troops to the Kishon River and give him into your hands."

---

Give everything you are dealing with over to God. Battles are not meant to be fought alone. They are the Lord's. He will be there every step of the way.

### Jabin - discerner

Jabin thought he knew how to oppress the people of Israel, but God was and is always the wiser. He was familiar with the people, however, he was not familiar with their God. Similarly, people do not understand the power of God within each of us. On a mission to destroy our character, they will be turned around because we are made new in Him, daily. You cannot destroy what God makes anew.

There are people who know how to push your buttons. They know what makes you happy, sad, and angry. Do not allow them to have power over you. Turn the other cheek (Matthew 5:39) and prove they do not know you as well as God, your Father, knows you.

When others seek to harm you, how do you respond? How are others encouraged to know more about the God in you?

_____

_____

_____

_____

_____

_____

_____

_____

_____

_____

_____

_____

_____

_____

_____

_____

## *Kishon – sore, cold, hard, and callous*

God has given us free will to flow, like a river, in whatever direction we choose. It is much easier to flow, however, when you have a sense of direction. Allowing life's current to flow wherever it pleases will only cause you to drown. Take charge of whirlwinds in your life by crying aloud for help, as did the people of Israel (Exodus 2:23). God saves when there is seemingly no way out of chaos. He throws a life jacket of grace and picks you up in a boat called love. You will never be saved if you don't shoot the flare of repentance. You become sore and numb to the pain of swimming in circles, only to circle back to the same place you thought you swam so hard to evade.

Give every life matter to God. He does not want you to take the journey without Him. You are not strong enough to bear the weight of the world. God sends help, but you must accept you cannot do life on your own. Acknowledge your help comes from Him.

## How can you allow God to flow through your life more smoothly?

_____

_____

_____

_____

_____

_____

_____

_____

_____

_____

_____

_____

_____

_____

_____

# Judges 4:8 (NIV)

Barak said to her, "If you go with me, I will go;
but if you don't go with me, I won't go."

Your journey should not be dependent on
that of others. Stop depending on others to
go with you to a place only you can go. God
intentionally places people in our lives to help
push and encourage us to continue. If they
stop pushing, however, you must continue to
push through and trust God.

### *If you go with me, I will go; but if you do not go with me, I will not go*

A Barak is an indecisive person who does not
fear the Lord. They rely on others to tell them
who God is. Beware of indecisive people. There
is a difference between mindful people and
those who have nothing in mind. Leave them
alone. Connect to a God who will never leave
you hanging, indecisively. He will always tell
you what you need to hear and knows the
direction of the relationship between you and
Him.

Run when you see a Barak coming your way.
Do not look back or you too may turn into
a pillar of salt (Genesis 19:26); a being with

no substance or value. Do not be salt, but rather soul food, a vessel that is complete and knows its worth. Be a Deborah, one willing to lead a Barak to Christ without compromising integrity or character.

James 1:8 warns a double-minded man is unstable. How can you increase your confidence in the Lord?

_____

_____

_____

_____

_____

_____

_____

_____

_____

_____

_____

_____

_____

_____

_____

_____

# GROW WITH GRACE

God gave Deborah a helpmate, a regular man who wore grace well. Lappidoth allowed the Holy Spirit to use him to impart insight to Deborah. To serve the Kingdom, you do not have to be well-known or recognized by multitudes. You only need to be someone willing to allow God to use you as He chooses. Ordinary people can do incredible things in the rapture of God. His grace sets you apart and sets you up for miracles.

## Judges 4:9 (NIV)

---

"Certainly, I will go with you," said Deborah. "But because of the course you are taking, the honor will not be yours, for the Lord will deliver Sisera into the hands of a woman." So, Deborah went with Barak to Kedesh."

---

If you are not a willing vessel, God will raise someone else up to do as He instructed you to do.

*Certainly – unquestionable; without the shadow of a doubt*

Deborah was ready to go into battle no matter the outcome. She put others first and went to war on behalf of the people of God. She trusted in the Word of God.

We must intercede and go to war on behalf of others. Many times, however, we question things that God ask us to do because it sounds 'crazy' or because we are fearful of the outcome. Fear is crippling and slows the plan God has for our lives. There are people who wait on us to step out on Faith and practice selflessness. Get out of your comfort zone, and on a path of generosity.

Are you selfless or selfish? How do you demonstrate intercession for others?

_____

_____

_____

_____

_____

_____

_____

_____

_____

_____

_____

_____

_____

_____

_____

_____

_____

_____

_____

_____

Deborah went into battle knowing she faced death, persecution, and rejection. God faced persecution, rejection, and death just the same. We are made in His image and His likeness, and we too will face challenges (Genesis 1:27). In times of trouble, remember, if God made it through, He shall help us persevere. According to Matthew 5:11, "Men shall revile you, and persecute you, and shall say all manner of evil against you falsely, for my sake." As our Father, He will see His children through. God is with us even unto the end of the world (Matthew 28:20).

Like Deborah, we cannot instruct the people of God to do something we have not done or would not do ourselves when instructed. We must lead by example, so others follow us as we follow Christ (1 Corinthians 11:1). People cannot follow us, however, if we do not trust in God and the power of His Word. If we knew who He was and is, we would not question Him, but rather reverence Him.

When will you stop asking why and start being the reason why? Why do you question God?

_____

_____

_____

_____

_____

_____

_____

_____

_____

_____

_____

_____

_____

_____

_____

_____

_____

_____

The same power in Him lives in us. We must seek His face for revelation and God will grant us that which we request (1 Chronicles 4:10). God loves us unconditionally, and yet we conditionally love Him. If He answers our prayers, we praise Him. Do something different. Praise Him in advance for what is coming. Continue even when He does not seem to answer.

Do you praise God when it is convenient? Or, do you praise your way through the inconveniences of life?

_____

_____

_____

_____

_____

_____

_____

_____

_____

_____

_____

_____

_____

_____

_____

_____

_____

_____

## *Course - progress without distraction*

God wants to take us to new dimensions in Him. The story of Deborah provides great insight on how to get there. God always keeps His promises to us, but we must first do what is required of us. Because Barak depended on the relationship Deborah had with God, God would not allow her words to fall void. However, Barak would not receive honor because he did not have a relationship with God for himself.

Identify areas in your life where you can honor God in obedience.

_____

_____

_____

_____

_____

_____

_____

_____

_____

_____

_____

_____

_____

_____

_____

_____

_____

_____

Barak questioned God, thus not able to move from a place of bondage. Many times, we lead our lives where we feel we will prosper, keeping busy and distracted. Many people get stuck in the same place because they refuse to trust. Barak gave up the right to receive a spiritual or physical promotion because he was crippled with fear and distrust. God wants to promote us to new levels in Him, but promotion does not come without sacrifice.

Have you been stuck in the same place? What are you going to do to get unstuck?

_____

_____

_____

_____

_____

_____

_____

_____

_____

_____

_____

_____

_____

_____

_____

_____

_____

_____

_____

_____

### Honor – righteous, justice, and fairness

Deborah's ability to judge and render just decisions caused people from all walks of life to seek her. She presided over the people's court as an honorable judge. In life, you want to stand as one who provides insight, speaks with wisdom, and gives instruction led by the Holy Spirit.

Barak's name meant lighting and thunder. With such a name, you would expect Barak to command attention. However, Barak was unaware, as a lot of us are, to the full measure of God's power working in and through him. He refused to look beyond the success he experienced because he thought things could not get any better. A lot of times, we do the same. We refuse to look beyond battles God wants us to conquer.

What are some examples of your honorable lifestyle? How do you show humility?

_____

_____

_____

_____

_____

_____

_____

_____

_____

_____

_____

_____

_____

_____

_____

_____

We must live up to our names; daughters and sons of God. Honor goes deeper than name recognition. Others will honor and respect you when they recognize God in you and the power you hold as His child. Honor comes from God, and God alone.

Who does God say you are (John 1:12)? What do you say about who God is (Mark 8:27-30)?

_____

_____

_____

_____

_____

_____

_____

_____

_____

_____

_____

_____

_____

_____

_____

_____

_____

_____

_____

### Deliver – to bring out of bondage

Instead of giving the assignment to Barak, God assigned Jael to kill Sisera. In God's sight, Barak did not deserve honor. God delivered Sisera into the hands of a woman, and He will deliver us to a reprobate mind if we do not seek His will (Romans1:28).

Disobedience and fear are not rewarded in the Kingdom. God will raise up others to do what He asked you to do if you are not obedient. A spirit of conviction should overtake you when God shows you where you could have been. Willingness and obedience to God's instructions will take you further than you can imagine.

Are you going to step up and claim what is rightfully yours as an heir of God (Romans 8:17)? Will you be delivered and set free, or delivered to a reprobate mind?

_____

_____

_____

_____

_____

_____

_____

_____

_____

_____

_____

_____

_____

_____

### *Hands - powerful instrument that was given to us by God to be used for His purpose*

God blessed you with hands. It is imperative you be mindful of who you touch and who you allow to touch you. Be careful about the work your hands stir. Handle others with care and be intentional in your interactions to help those in need. Pray for the weak and weary. Speak in the lives of people who seemingly lack hope. Tap into your potential to unlock potential in someone else. Walk like you can help others reach their purpose. You are that powerful. But, you must believe you were born equipped to effect change in the lives of others.

If you are blessed with the gift of healing hands, act with power and grace, instructed by the Father. Ensure your heart is pure and behave accordingly.

How do you choose to use your hands or words? When have you healed? When have you done harm?

_____

_____

_____

_____

_____

_____

_____

_____

_____

_____

_____

_____

_____

_____

_____

_____

_____

_____

_____

## *Woman – a female that has matured and transitioned into being a daughter of God*

God values His daughters. He will use women as He chooses, if we will follow instructions and are obedient to His commands. As a female judge, Deborah allowed God to use her. This was rare during that period. God used Jael, a mighty woman, to silence her enemy. He used Queen Esther to deliver the Jews from the hands of death (Esther 4:14). God, our Father, will use His daughters whenever, wherever, and however, if we are willing. Willing vessels are sold-out to every will of God. Unwilling vessels sell out to the world.

## Are you a sell-out or are you sold out?

_____

_____

_____

_____

_____

_____

_____

_____

_____

_____

_____

_____

_____

_____

_____

_____

_____

_____

_____

Deborah could have been afraid to die in battle. Jael could have been afraid that Sisera would kill her. Queen Esther could have been afraid of a death sentence. All three women walked out of sensitive circumstances untouched and victorious. If they could face death, why are we afraid of persecution or rejection from outsiders? We have no excuses.

Unbelievers and those weak in faith wait for us to reveal who God is through us. People around you may be spiritually dying because you have not. We walk through the valley of the shadow of death daily but should not fear evil. Instead, find comfort in God (Psalm 23:4). Fear is a painful emotion brought on by the expectation of evil. The Bible encourages those who trust in the Lord to expect good things from Him (Psalm 62:5). He will never let you down, despite disappointments you suffer at the hands of your enemies.

What do you expect from God? What does God expect from you?

_____

_____

_____

_____

_____

_____

_____

_____

_____

_____

_____

_____

_____

_____

_____

_____

It is said you never realize how much strength a woman has until it comes to protecting those she loves. Jael knew Sisera posed a threat to her family and her way of life, so she killed him as God instructed.

We must be willing to kill bad relationships, bad habits, bad thoughts, and bad attitudes. Eliminate things in your life that keep you from moving forward. Sin seeps into your home and your heart, just like Sisera slipped his way into Jael's tent. When you identify the enemy, be willing to rid yourself of it no matter what it takes. If you are not willing to do all God has commanded you to do, you will not get all He has for you. God commands us to be strong and courageous (Joshua 1:9). Do not worry about the future because tomorrow has enough troubles (Matthew 6:34).

What are you willing to kill to have peace in your home and in your life?

_____

_____

_____

_____

_____

_____

_____

_____

_____

_____

_____

_____

_____

_____

_____

_____

_____

_____

# Judges 4:10 (NIV)

---

"There Barak summoned Zebulun and Naphtali, and ten thousand men went up under his command. Deborah also went up with Him."

---

God will align you with unlikely allies to help win souls in the battle for the Kingdom. We are stronger together than apart.

### Summon – to appear by command

God gave Barak yet another opportunity to take charge and do something he should have done. Even after our disobedience, God will give us opportunities to do as He instruct.

"Then Samson prayed to the Lord, "Sovereign Lord, remember me. Please, God, strengthen me just once more, and let me with one blow get revenge on the Philistines for my two eyes" (Judges 16:28 NIV). If both Samson and Barak had done as instructed, they would not have been in predicaments that lingered. However, merciful God gave them one more chance to get it right. Whether you are on your deathbed or well and able to do as God has instructed, Sovereign God is a God of many chances.

Will God summon you more than once? Or, will you answer when first summoned?

_____

_____

_____

_____

_____

_____

_____

_____

_____

_____

_____

_____

_____

_____

_____

_____

_____

### *Zebulun- a gift & Naphtali- the struggle*

Struggle is a gift. The gifts are lessons learned because of struggle. Struggle brings people together and makes us relatable. God will draw people together from various backgrounds to fight alongside Him in the battle to win souls. We all struggle in similar ways. Christ is within all of us, but does not force our decisions. God is everywhere and in everything. If you look only to what and who you know, you may miss Him. United we stand, divided we fall.

## Do you struggle with your God given gift(s)? How, or why?

_____

_____

_____

_____

_____

_____

_____

_____

_____

_____

_____

_____

_____

_____

_____

_____

### Went up –spiritually and physically elevated

God promoted Deborah to a higher place because of her willingness to be who He needed her to be at the moment. She was a prophet and judge to all. Still, God added to her the title of a warrior. Who you are is already in you. Unless you answer the call on your life, you will not know you have everything you need to succeed. As you become more willing, God adds more to your plate. He will never put more on you than you can bear (1 Corinthians 10:13).

## How are you preparing for a promotion?

_____

_____

_____

_____

_____

_____

_____

_____

_____

_____

_____

_____

_____

_____

_____

_____

_____

_____

# Judges 4:11 (NIV)

---

"Now Heber the Kenite had left the other Kenites, the descendants of Hobab, Moses' brother-in-law, and pitched his tent by the great tree in Zaanannim near Kedesh."

---

When God tells you to move, move without question. There is great reward in obedience.

### Heber - to easily pass over

The battle passed over Heber and his family because he moved where God told Him to move. Just because you are inside the will of God, does not mean you will not face trials and tribulations. Because you are inside of His will, trials and tribulations are that much easier to bear. You are not alone in your walk with God.

You may find unpleasant events happening around you, but experience peace. In the story of Moses, God sent ten plagues that included locusts, diseased livestock, and the death of the firstborns. The Egyptians experienced the plagues while the Hebrews waited until the day Pharaoh released them. Along with the last plague came instructions to put blood on the doors to avoid the death of firstborn children (Exodus 12:7-13).

God will give you instructions on how to prepare for the storms of life, but you must do what He asks to remain protected. Whether you are Heber and God tells you to move, or you are Moses and He instructs you to swipe blood over the door, you must follow God's voice. Do what is necessary to maintain a sound mind, peace, and joy.

When trouble comes, will you allow it to pass
over, or take you in a direction away from God?
What are you willing to do to secure your place
in God's Kingdom?

_____

_____

_____

_____

_____

_____

_____

_____

_____

_____

_____

_____

_____

_____

_____

_____

### Kenites – craftsman and blacksmith

Heber was a Kenite, and well-connected to other Kenites. Sometimes in life, however, we must leave our friends (what we know) and family (familiarity) behind so we can hear from God. Cut ties with distractions that seek to take you away from Him. Heber left people who were seemingly hard workers. Hard work for the sake of accomplishment does not get you into the Kingdom. The accomplishment of Kingdom-minded goals, with the right heart posture, grants you access to His Kingdom.

Are you hardly working for the Kingdom, while 'working hard' for man?

_____

_____

_____

_____

_____

_____

_____

_____

_____

_____

_____

_____

_____

_____

### *Hobab – to be loved*

Because of who you are, God will spare your family.

God spared Lot and his two daughters because of Abraham's request. "So, it was that, when God destroyed the cities of the valley, God remembered Abraham and sent Lot out of the midst of the overthrow when he overthrew the cities in which Lot had lived" (Genesis 19:29). Abraham wanted to see his family protected from God's wrath.

Kenites came from Hobab, a beloved man of God. His descendants, however, had no interest in the things of God. God spared them from war because of the seed of obedience sown in previous generations. It is important to leave a good legacy for your children and your children's children. "A good man leaves behind an inheritance, but a sinner's wealth is stored up for the righteous" (Proverbs 13:22).

## What legacy are you building?

_____

_____

_____

_____

_____

_____

_____

_____

_____

_____

_____

_____

_____

_____

_____

_____

_____

_____

### Zaanannim – to be asleep

You will experience great peace inside the will of God. Good rest will find you and overtake you. When you are outside His will, you experience feelings of anguish, discontentment, and emptiness.

Would you rather experience restless sleep, or a peaceful rest that surpasses all understanding (Philippians 4:7)?

_____

_____

_____

_____

_____

_____

_____

_____

_____

_____

_____

_____

_____

_____

_____

_____

# Judges 4:12 (NIV)

"When they told Sisera that Barak son of Abinoam had gone up to Mount Tabor,"

Let no man try to stop what God ordains. It may seem as though your enemies are getting over on you, but they set up circumstances for your comeback.

*They*

They can represent anyone who waits for your downfall or wish you malice. Everyone will not express excitement for your enthusiasm about Christ. Believe it or not, some people may try to sabotage your next moves. Everything happens for a reason. He will work it out in your favor.

Although they (the people) informed Sisera of Barak's next move, Sisera would not have been in the right place at the right time to slip into Jaels' tent. You cannot mess up Gods' Holy and perfect plan no matter how hard you try. Do not attempt to interrupt God's plans. His name is glorious whether or not you are used. It is better to be on God's team when the dust settles.

Think of a time someone intended something for your bad. How did God turn it around for your good?

_____

_____

_____

_____

_____

_____

_____

_____

_____

_____

_____

_____

_____

_____

_____

_____

### *Abinoam - a kind father*

Barak did not follow God's instructions. But, because his earthly father was obedient, the blessings and favor of God flowed to Him. Awareness of who you are connected to is important whether in friendships or familial ties.

Barak was identified by his father. Will people be able to identify you in relation to your Father?

_____

_____

_____

_____

_____

_____

_____

_____

_____

_____

_____

_____

_____

_____

_____

_____

_____

## Tabor – high places

God may place you at untouchable heights, but do not forget that He placed you there. He can lift you up, or allow you to fall. Untouchable does not mean you are better than anyone else. Untouchable signifies no one can replicate the relationship you have with your heavenly Father. Many fail because they try replicate what they see in the natural. They do not realize you must rely on God's strength and the Holy Spirit. Battles are spiritual, not natural. You are first elevated spiritually. Spiritual elevation manifests itself in the natural.

Are you focused on the spiritual and eternal things of God, or the natural and temporary things of this world?

_____

_____

_____

_____

_____

_____

_____

_____

_____

_____

_____

_____

_____

_____

_____

_____

# Judges 4:13 (NIV)

---

"Sisera summoned from Harosheth Haggoyim to the Kishon River all his men and his nine hundred chariots fitted with iron."

---

No place is too impenetrable for God to enter. No man is too high for God to reach. No earthly army is too large for God to defeat. Stop seeing things in the natural and believe God for the supernatural.

### Summon – to appear by command

Just because someone calls, does not mean you have to answer. Yes, you have been anointed by God to speak life, help others in need, and to serve. But God also gives you wisdom. Pick your battles, using Godly wisdom. While it is important to take a stand against evildoings (Psalm 94:16), sometimes you must let others make mistakes. If they heed your warnings concerning their choices, continue to follow-up and be a light.

Just as Barak summoned his men and they came running; we are called similarly to draw others to God through an exemplary life. People should want to know about God because of the life you live. They should desire to know how you got to where you are, and desire the life God has for them (Jeremiah 29:11). People should want to follow you as you follow Christ.

Many people will do almost anything to experience peace and feelings of self-worth. Often, we seek these feelings from outside sources instead of going straight to the Source. Lead others to the Source and they will find all they want and need in Him. Before you can lead others, however, you must first follow. "Come with me. I'll make a new kind of fisherman out of you. I'll show you how to catch men and women instead of perch and bass" (Matthew 4:19-20 MSG).

Are you a good leader or a better follower? Do you know when to lead and when to follow?

_____

_____

_____

_____

_____

_____

_____

_____

_____

_____

_____

_____

_____

_____

_____

_____

_____

_____

### Harosheth Haggoyim – Sisera's fortress

Know when to guard your heart, and when to lower your guard. Guard your heart concerning worldly things and people. Allow God to have His way in your life. There is nothing wishy-washy about the body of Christ, and as a fellow citizen of the Kingdom you should not be. Be as strong as a fortress concerning the Word of God. "For the word of God is alive and active. Sharper than any double-edged sword, it penetrates even to dividing soul and spirit, joints and marrow" (Hebrews 4:12). Spend time in the Word and allow the things of God to remain in your heart.

Once a wall is down, anything can enter. Guarding your heart allows happiness, joy, and peace of mind. The unguarded are often victims. Guard your heart and remain vigilant in the Word of God. Be watchful. The devil, your adversary, seeks to seeks to kill, steal, and destroy (John 10:10).

How do you guard your heart from the enemy?
Discuss a time when you unwisely lowered your
guard.

_____

_____

_____

_____

_____

_____

_____

_____

_____

_____

_____

_____

_____

_____

_____

_____

*'All his men and his nine hundred chariots fitted with iron.'*

It may seem as if the world is against you. Remember, we do not fight against flesh and blood, but spiritual forces (Ephesians 6:120). You are 'fit' with all you need to fight against advances of the world. The world may seem to have all it needs to bring you down, but you are a powerful force. When you realize your power, you will take the world by storm (1 John 4:4).

As an employee at a technologically advanced defense company, I learned about weapons designed to keep our enemies guessing and at bay. Weapons and their capabilities can be intimidating. In the Scriptures, however, "The weapons of our warfare are not carnal, but mighty through God to the pulling down of strong holds" (2 Corinthians 10:4 KJV). The weapons of our spiritual warfare are mightier than the weapons we build.

**Weapons of spiritual warfare:**

1. **Prayer and worship.** Prayer is the open line of communication between you and your Heavenly Father. God answers prayers. In His presence, you can find all you need. Prayer begins the process of cementing the groundwork and worship solidifies the foundation laid by Jesus

Christ (1Corinthians 3:11). You cannot
fight on rocky ground.

2. **The Word of God.** We cannot fight the
weapons of spiritual warfare through
intellect, but by every Word God speaks
(Matthew 4:4). To fight the good fight
of faith without nourishment of the
Word of God, is to lose the fight before
it starts. Put on the whole armor of God
(Ephesians 6:11). Without protection, you
may be persuaded to join the other side.

3. **The Holy Spirit.** The Holy Spirit is
obsolete without prayer, worship, and
the Word. Prayer invites Him into your
life, worship allows you to hear. The
Word brings confirmation to what you
hear in this season. Not everyone's
battle is meant to be fought and not
everyone can be won over by words
or actions. The Holy Spirit ensures you
fight the right battle, for the right cause,
all for His glory. The Holy Spirit, sent by
God the Father, will instruct you and help
bring all things to your remembrance
(John 14:26).

4. **The Power of your testimony.** Everyone
has a season of trials and tribulations;
it is important to reassure others they
are not alone. If God brought you out,
He will do the same for others. Do not

be ashamed of your testimony and do not be afraid to tell others of God's goodness (2 Timothy 1:8). You cannot bring people to Christ if you do not know how you obtained salvation.

5. **Fasting.** Fasting allows you to hear more clearly from God concerning your purpose. Fasting for a specified time to fill up on the Word of God is beneficial. A fast from social media and matters of the world allows space to learn what God says about you and unlearn what the world desires of you. Solitude helps gain insight and vision into what is going on in your life and the world around you. Move away from distractions. Allow yourself time to hear from God. Understand why you fast, whether to loosen the bands of wickedness (Isaiah 58:5-6), or to heal yourself and others (2 Samuel 12:15-17). Whatever reason the Holy Spirit leads you to fast, be sure not to show it on your countenance or make it your disposition so that everyone is aware (Matthew 6:16-18).

*This information is intended as general insight and should not be treated as advice. Please consult a physician before fasting.

How do you build yourself up in God's Word?
Make a plan to strengthen the time you spend
with God.

_____

_____

_____

_____

_____

_____

_____

_____

_____

_____

_____

_____

_____

_____

_____

_____

# Judges 4:14 (NIV)

---

"Then Deborah said to Barak, "Go! This is the day the LORD has given Sisera into your hands. Has not the LORD gone ahead of you?" So, Barak went down Mount Tabor, with ten thousand men following Him."

---

God makes our paths clear. Step out on faith and behold a victorious walk with Christ; not only for you, but many others.

### Has not the LORD gone ahead of you?

When someone goes ahead of you, he or she makes the path clear and a little easier for you to travel. God will always make a way for you when there is seemingly no way. Many times, we do not follow the path God has laid out for us because it requires faith. Walking with God is a faith walk. "Now faith is the substance of things hoped for, the evidence of things not seen" (Hebrews 11:1 KJV).

We stick to what we know instead of stepping out on faith because we have no clue as to the life God has in store for us. God will always give you a glimpse of where He is taking you. However, sometimes we are not able to receive revelations concerning our future because we focus on the present or mistakes of the past. So many people are afraid of greatness. They would rather stick to what they know and remain mediocre rather than take a faith walk and become great in the Lord.

Will you trust, believe, and continue the good fight of faith? Or, will you live in fear and completely miss the mark?

_____
_____
_____
_____
_____
_____
_____
_____
_____
_____
_____
_____
_____
_____
_____
_____

When a woman or man of God steps out on faith and speaks into your life, you must step out on faith to receive the Word. To refute the Word of God and not take heed, is to make a liar of God. Speaking into someone's life requires great faith. To receive a Word requires even more. Believe God will manifest Himself in your life in due time. He will get the glory.

## What has God's Word spoken to you? What will you do with the information you received?

_____

_____

_____

_____

_____

_____

_____

_____

_____

_____

_____

_____

_____

_____

_____

_____

# Judges 4:15 (NIV)

---

"At Barak's advance, the Lord routed Sisera
and all his chariots and army by the sword,
and Sisera got down from his chariot and
fled on foot."

---

Outside God's will, you may encounter a
whirlwind of chaos. Pay attention to the signs.
Get back on track, or ignore the warning signs
and be lost forever. The choice is yours.

*Advance – to purposefully move forward;
progress in all aspects of life*

To improve your life in all areas, move further
into the things of God. Advancement in the
Kingdom not only helps you find purpose, but
helps others find their purpose. Stagnation
affects everyone around you. We are called
to uplift others and encourage them to move
forward purposefully. When we play church,
others may be led astray. Advance so others
around you are affected positively. It is selfish
for you to remain in the same place for years.
The destiny of others is connected to your
assignment in the Earth.

How will you advance in the Kingdom of God? Remember, you are either digressing or progressing.

_____

_____

_____

_____

_____

_____

_____

_____

_____

_____

_____

_____

_____

_____

_____

_____

### *Routed – confused, chaotic, and disorganized*

"The way of transgressors is hard" (Proverbs 13:15 KJV). When you go against the will of God, you will feel like your life is thrown into a world of chaos and confusion. Your spiritual life is reflected in your physical life. A chaotic spirit will manifest itself and bring to light an unorganized life and unclean home. God gives clarity as we press towards Him. Clarity comes by transformation of a renewed mind (Romans 12:2). Confusion comes from closed off and adverse thoughts. God says, "For my thoughts are not your thoughts, neither are your ways my ways," (Isaiah 55:8 NIV). In the flesh, we are averse to God's way of thinking. If you ask the Lord to renew your mindset and help you change your ways, you will prosper. Allow Him to guide you through clarity.

Do you find yourself routed like Sisera? How clear are you about God's direction in your life?

_____

_____

_____

_____

_____

_____

_____

_____

_____

_____

_____

_____

_____

_____

_____

_____

_____

### Fled on foot - to run away from

Stop running away from God. Answer the call now, or answer on judgment day. Answer now and breathe a sigh of relief rather than be denied by your Father in Heaven. "But whoever disowns me before others, I will disown before my Father in heaven" (Matthew 10:33 NIV).

Through Sisera, it is evident some decisions may be a matter of life and death. The further away you move from God, the closer you are to death. If you try to save your own life, you will lose it. If you lose your life for God, He will save you (Matthew 16:25). Sisera tried to save his life by running away, but Jael put an end to him. Deborah was willing to lose her life in battle and was saved by the grace of God. Run away from God, and you will run into danger. Instead, run into His arms. There you will find love, compassion, forgiveness, and grace.

Some people run away from the Body of Christ because they fear judgement. "Therefore, there is now no condemnation for those who are in Christ Jesus" (Romans 8:1 NIV). As Believers, we must do a better job to encourage those who seek salvation. They are often pushed away by our bad attitudes and standoffish demeanor. Those who judge should seek Christ with more diligence.

Who or what will you run towards? Who or what will you run away from?

_____

_____

_____

_____

_____

_____

_____

_____

_____

_____

_____

_____

_____

_____

# Judges 4:16 (NIV)

"Barak pursued the chariots and army as far as Harosheth Haggoyim, and all Sisera's troops fell by the sword; not a man was left."

At some point, we have all found ourselves with our backs against the wall. This is the place where God desires for us to be. It is in this place of vulnerability that He can reach us.

### Pursue – *To passionately follow*

To reach the brighter side of God's promise, persevere through the dark storms of life. Chase God with a vision of where He is taking you. He will show you if you ask, but do not blindly chase without a sense of purpose. Without vision, you will feel as if you are going in circles and eventually stop chasing (Proverbs 29:18). When you receive God's revelation for your life, share His goodness with others. We cannot make the mistake of neglecting to bring others along in our quest for Christ (Esther 4:14 NIV). Chase those who struggle with their purpose. God will give you wisdom during your pursuit to win souls for the Kingdom.

Are you willing to persevere to get all God has for you? Or, do you give up at the first sign of trouble?

_____

_____

_____

_____

_____

_____

_____

_____

_____

_____

_____

_____

_____

_____

_____

_____

## As far as – for as great as

As far as the things of God are concerned, how far are you willing to go to fulfill Kingdom-purpose? God will never ask you to do anything He does not equip you to do. Put on your spiritual mind, eyes, and ears to understand you can handle any tasks God asks of you. If He instructs you to leave your job to pursue full-time ministry, will you say yes? If He tells you to pray with your enemy, will you say yes? If He commands you to deliver a different message on Sunday morning than the one you prepared on Saturday night, will you adapt and say yes? Whatever God asks you to do, will you say yes? The phrase 'as far as' has no limits. He will take you as far as you are willing to go.

What limits have you placed on your life? What are you going to do to reach a place in God where there are no limits?

_____

_____

_____

_____

_____

_____

_____

_____

_____

_____

_____

_____

_____

_____

_____

_____

### *Fell by the sword – The Word of God*

It is important for us to stay in the Word. Study the Word of God to gain a new meaning to a life inside His will (2 Timothy 2:15). However, do not expect the Word to take effect if you do not do your part. If you want God to have His way in your life, seek His face for revelations. Equip yourself with the Armor of God. The Word is like a mirror; it is the only principle by which you should govern yourself and adjust accordingly. If you study the Word and your lifestyle does not match up, re-evaluate your choices and live by the Word.

Do you resemble the contents of God's Word?
Or, are you the evidence of an unopened Word?

_____

_____

_____

_____

_____

_____

_____

_____

_____

_____

_____

_____

_____

_____

_____

_____

_____

## Not a man was left

Either get left behind, or leave others behind. God gave us free will, but choose wisely. You can opt to watch as life passes you by or take part in the things of God. Left behind has nothing to do with the end times. It concerns negligence of the body of Christ for the things of the world.

Will you get left behind, or will you leave others behind?

_____

_____

_____

_____

_____

_____

_____

_____

_____

_____

_____

_____

_____

_____

_____

_____

# GLOW IN GLORY

Deborah sat under a tree, and the Bible says people from all over sought her out for counsel. In this life, glory is redeemed as others seek you for your calling. Others will hear of your gifts, grace, and honor.

## Judges 4:17 (NIV)

"Sisera, meanwhile, fled on foot to the tent of Jael, the wife of Heber the Kenite, because there was an alliance between Jabin king of Hazor and the family of Heber the Kenite."

When we run into the arms of anyone other than God, the result is grave danger.

### Meanwhile – the wait

Often, God waits for us to come to Him. When we wait to receive an answer from God, we must "Wait on the Lord and be of good courage" (Psalm 27:14 KJV). God works on our behalf and sets us up better than we could imagine. If you abort the process, the results of impatience will be an incomplete spiritual life and a broken relationship with your Heavenly Father. The process is necessary and well worth the wait. Success does not come overnight. But because you are inside His way, He may quicken the process.

## Will you wait on God? Or, is God waiting on you?

_____

_____

_____

_____

_____

_____

_____

_____

_____

_____

_____

_____

_____

_____

_____

_____

_____

_____

### Tent – A temporary dwelling

Is your house ready for visitors? Is your house strong enough to receive your enemies? Is your house compassionate enough to receive the weak and broken? Is your house a place where you desire God to dwell? If the answer to any of these questions is no, you have built in vain (Psalm 127:1). Allow God to dwell within your house, and He will build a welcome mat for salvation. When God dwells with you, you are positioned to encounter and conquer.

Is your house built strong enough to withstand the test of time?

_____

_____

_____

_____

_____

_____

_____

_____

_____

_____

_____

_____

_____

_____

_____

_____

_____

*Alliance - a uniting of like-minded individuals for a singular purpose.*

It is important to align yourselves with individuals who have a Kingdom-mindset. There is strength in numbers. The more you fellowship with other Believers in Christ, the more you will realize there are others who are where you are at the present time. Besides others who have been where you are and can provide guidance, there are those who desire to be where you are and need your help. Enemies will see where you are and leave you there; allies will see where you are, pick you up, dust you off, and help you on your way.

You may consider yourself an ally, but even the slightest disobedience and resistance to God's plan can slow progress. There are no gray areas in ministry, and the battle is too important for anyone to find themselves in between the fight for good and evil. Allies are others who you can confide in and expect not to sabotage your efforts. If you do not have allies, re-evaluate the company you keep. Allies are not only friends but confidants, protectors, and brothers and sisters. "A friend loves at all times, and a brother is born for a time of adversity" (Proverbs 17:17 NIV).

Who do you consider an ally? Who would consider you an ally?

_____

_____

_____

_____

_____

_____

_____

_____

_____

_____

_____

_____

_____

_____

_____

### Familiarity (family) – a false sense of acquaintance with people or certain subject matters

Familiarity can be good or bad. There is familiarity that will get you in trouble, and familiarity that will set you up for a blessing. In Sisera's case, he thought he could trust Heber's family. For many, familiarity is breeding grounds for disrespect. Just because people know you, it does not mean they have your best interest at heart. When you run to others, rather than God first, you risk danger. Familiarity with the Heber family caused Sisera to become comfortable, lower his guard, and fall asleep.

Many times, we may not go to sleep physically, but we go to sleep spiritually and mentally. We are in a constant battle for our mind, body, and spirit. We cannot afford to bat an eye or 'not see' what is directly in front of us, or down the road. Never get too comfortable and forget to guard your heart. The Lord gives rest to His beloved (Psalms 127:2).

We must do our part to ensure we operate in a pure heart. Familiarity can stunt growth. For Sisera, a bad alliance turned out to be a good alliance for Jael. Align yourself with the wrong crowd, and you may find yourself in danger. Align yourself with the Word of God, and it will never steer you wrong.

Do you know God for yourself? Or, are you familiar with His goodness through others?

_____

_____

_____

_____

_____

_____

_____

_____

_____

_____

_____

_____

_____

_____

_____

# Judges 4:18 (NIV)

---

"Jael went out to meet Sisera and said to him,
"Come, my lord, come right in. Don't be afraid."
So, he entered her tent, and she covered him
with a blanket."

---

Beware of those who make it easy to enter their lives without question. Be careful of those you allow to enter your life without question. Guard your home and remind others to guard their own.

### Jael went out to meet Sisera

Greet your enemies with open arms. Kill them with kindness and a genuine sweet spirit. Love others with the love of God. To turn the other cheek does not seem practical to some, however, the love of God covers all. Pray for wisdom and allow the Holy Spirit to lead and guide you. Be triumphant over those who despitefully use you (Matthew 5:44).

Use Godly wisdom in dealing with family, friends, and acquaintances. You can be related to someone and not have a relationship with them and vice versa. Just as Jael went out to meet Sisera, greet your loved ones with open arms.

Who or what has entered your home and stolen what's important? How can you allow God to enter and restore the stolen?

_____

_____

_____

_____

_____

_____

_____

_____

_____

_____

_____

_____

_____

_____

### Come, my Lord

People should draw near to the Christ in us. Honor God's glory and anointing on your life. The anointing will cause people to be open and confide in you. When they do, do not condemn, but relay the Word of God to their situation. Rely on the Holy Spirit to guide your speech. Welcome the gift of the Holy Spirit in your life and accept that people will be attracted to the God in you. Recognize when the attraction is past the point of ungodliness and redirect them to Christ. If you face a situation where you are unsure, seek God and wise counsel from trusted individuals.

The journey is not traveled alone. While others may be open with you, you must be willing and able to expose fears. Silence brings grief and confusion, but transparency brings clarity and relief.

When have you taken life on alone, rather than admit you needed help? What was the result of your actions?

_____

_____

_____

_____

_____

_____

_____

_____

_____

_____

_____

_____

_____

_____

_____

_____

### She covered him with a blanket

Cover your enemies in prayer, cover your enemies with words of encouragement. Set others up to fall for God's love and salvation. God will either move your enemies out the way, or give you wisdom for victory. God desires to deliver those who want to bring you harm. Break the spirit of malice with kindness. No matter how hard naysayers try, they cannot make God's Word lie (Hebrews 1:13).

Will you cover your enemies in prayer? Or, will you allow naysayers to cover you in doubt, uncertainty, worry, and fear?

_____

_____

_____

_____

_____

_____

_____

_____

_____

_____

_____

_____

_____

_____

_____

_____

_____

# Judges 4:19 (NIV)

---

"I'm thirsty," he said. "Please give me some water." She opened a skin of milk, gave him a drink, and covered him up."

---

Choose wisely in what you ask for and note what is given. It is in Him we can find all we need.

### Thirsty - a desire for a need to be met

Often, danger comes in the form of flattery and charm, and will welcome you with open arms. If you find yourself brittle, like a plant with no water, you have not allowed God to shower you with His love. You may be thirsty for the approval of man rather than of God. There are moments in our lives when we all lack moisture and are hungry. The Bible tells us that "man shall not live on bread alone, but by every word that proceedeth out of the mouth of God" (Matthew 4:4 KJV). Lack may be a sign of disobedience. Fulfillment and worthiness are in Christ.

Reliance on things of the world results in a depleted emotional state and desire for more. Quench your thirst at the source of hydration. Visit God's well daily.

Who or what do you rely upon to quench your thirst for affection and the insatiable appetite for life? Is God enough for you?

_____

_____

_____

_____

_____

_____

_____

_____

_____

_____

_____

_____

_____

_____

_____

_____

_____

*She opened a skin of milk, gave him a drink, and covered him up.*

Jael could have completed one task for Sisera, but instead completed three. In the same manner, God has given us numerous gifts and talents to use for those in need. Our enemies direly need our love and grace; the same love and grace extended to us by Jesus Christ. Despite how you may see things, go above and beyond the call of duty to extend kindness. This is what Jesus did and Jael shows we can do.

According to Colossians 4:5-6, "Be wise in the way you act towards outsiders; make the most of every opportunity. Let your conversations be always full of grace, seasoned with salt, so that you may know how to answer everyone". Jael gave Sisera more than he asked because she wanted him to feel comfortable.

No matter your pursuits, you may encounter people who despise you. Do not allow negative comments or spiteful actions to deter you. Let your actions speak positive volumes. When naysayers realize your courageousness in the Lord, they will do just as Sisera did – lie down and rest. Leave no room for doubt about who you serve. The Word reminds us we cannot serve two masters (Matthew 6:24).

How do you go above and beyond to help those in need? Have you ever ignored a need of someone else? Why?

# Judges 4:20 (NIV)

---

"Stand in the doorway of the tent," he told her.
"If someone comes by and asks you,
'is anyone in there?' say 'No.'"

---

Do not compromise who you are for the betterment of someone else. You will be judged for your actions, regardless of the actions of others. Dishonesty will be judged.

### Stand – an upright position where one is at ease

Ministry requires you to be on the move. However, you must find a place of rest during it all. Ministry is comparable to standing, and it is better to stand than sit in the presence of God. Standing allows you to move quickly when He gives you instruction. Standing is also the universal symbol for respect. Sitting signifies fear and can often be viewed as disrespectful. Sitting gives you the option to remain inactive and dormant. Every one of us is a volcano waiting to erupt with the revelation of who God says we are. God does not give us much room to be disobedient. Be ready to move when the opportunity presents itself.

## Will you be standing or sitting when God returns?

_____

_____

_____

_____

_____

_____

_____

_____

_____

_____

_____

_____

_____

_____

_____

_____

## *Is anyone in there?*

Answer the door when God knocks. If a friend knocks at your door, you would be excited to answer. When God knocks, most dread responding because we do not know what is in store. Why do we not allow God's entrance, but carry around so much baggage? We allow the things that drain us of energy and time while we refuse to accept things that restore strength and vitality.

Just as Jael was alert to Sisera, we should be on guard. When you allow someone into your home, make sure God enters. Even when we think we are alone; we are not. Keep yourself and your house covered in prayer. When others enter, they should be able to feel His presence. If you allow your Father to dwell, there will be no room for unequally yoked relationships. God is a jealous God (Exodus 34:14).

Identify baggage you carry. Make a plan to release and trust God.

# Judges 4:21 (NIV)

---

"But Jael, Heber's wife, picked up a tent peg
and a hammer and went quietly to him while
he lay fast asleep, exhausted. She drove the
peg through his temple into the ground,
and he died."

---

Sometimes we need to sit back, relax, and watch God unfold His plans. There is no reason to announce moves you make in Christ. There is nothing dishonest about discretion.

### Picked up a tent peg

Essentially, we need to evaluate what we will give up and put up with in ministry. If frustrated with ministering to someone who does not accept the Word, do you give up? Or, do you wait for God's instructions? If instructed to be patient through rebuke, will you be obedient? What are you willing to do, to lift a heavy burden?

Will you accept difficult assignments from God?
Will you labor even when you are tired?

_____

_____

_____

_____

_____

_____

_____

_____

_____

_____

_____

_____

_____

_____

_____

_____

_____

## *Went quietly to him*

God is such a gentleman. He will correct you in quiet and reassure you of His love (Psalm 91:1). Constructive criticism requires growth (Hebrews 12:6). Without it, you lack direction. If the journey you embarked on requires kicking, screaming, and arm-pulling, you may be on the wrong journey.

As God corrects you, correct others in the same manner. Do not put others on blast for the entire world to see. What is done in secret will come to light, and you will see the fruits of your labor. God desires to reward us, and the best reward is to witness when others bloom into their potential. It is a true blessing when someone no longer depends on the relationship you have with God but pursues a relationship with God for themselves. The greatest reward is not wealth or prosperity, but rather the saving of souls.

Do you accept the correction of God in grace?
Are you an example of disobedience?

_____

_____

_____

_____

_____

_____

_____

_____

_____

_____

_____

_____

_____

_____

_____

_____

# Judges 4:22 (NIV)

---

"Just then Barak came by in pursuit of Sisera,
and Jael went out to meet him. "Come," she said,
"I will show you the man you're looking for."
So, he went in with her, and there lay Sisera
with the tent peg through his temple—dead."

---

When God releases you, you can reveal your plans to others. If you reveal too soon, you risk infringement by others.

### Barak came by in pursuit of Sisera

The Word God gave you is for you and no one else. What is for others is for them. What God has for you is for you only. We mess up when we try to follow instructions God gave to someone else. Follow the instructions you were given. God knows what you can handle. If you carry out someone else's instructions, you are disobedient. Disobedience fosters confusion.

Barak chased someone who was promised to someone else. Do not pursue a man or woman God promised to someone else. Be cautious not to allow someone else's blessing to impact your actions. Wait on God.

Will you receive what God has for you? Or, will you covet what others have in their lives?

_____

_____

_____

_____

_____

_____

_____

_____

_____

_____

_____

_____

_____

_____

_____

_____

# Judges 4:23 (NIV)

"On that day, God subdued Jabin king of Canaan before the Israelites."

God will move enemies out the way, but be willing to go through the fire to experience the rain. Wait on God to show up on your behalf.

### Subdue – *To force into submission*

If deemed necessary, God will subdue you. When you wreak havoc in your life and the lives of others, God will put a stop to it. God wants you to know and experience a greater life. Say yes to His will, mercy, and grace. God knows the desires of your heart. Your actions concerning His instructions give insight to how you view God.

The longer you linger to come to God, the harder it is to rid fleshly desires. God sees all you do. Be honest, transparent, and open about your desires.

What are your heart's desires? Are you willing to subdue all things that hinder your submission to Christ?

_____

_____

_____

_____

_____

_____

_____

_____

_____

_____

_____

_____

_____

_____

_____

_____

_____

# Judges 4:24 (NIV)

---

"And the hand of the Israelites pressed harder and harder against Jabin, king of Canaan until they destroyed him."

---

God will allow others to notice injustices you suffer. Others may even intercede on your behalf. God wants to deliver you untainted and untouched.

### Israelites

"But I tell you, do not resist an evil person. If anyone slaps you on the right cheek, turn to them the other cheek also" (Matthew 5:39 KJV). Your best weapon against injustices of this world is prayer and the Word. Emersion in God's Word allows you to know what He says about you, and prayer allows God to reconfirm who you are in Him. Be the same person God called you to be today and always. Others watch you and what you do.

Are your eyes fixed on people or are your eyes fixed on God? How can you discern the difference?

_____

_____

_____

_____

_____

_____

_____

_____

_____

_____

_____

_____

_____

_____

## Pressed harder

Continue to push despite all that is going on around you. While we have heard this advice a million times, we often try to push through on our strength alone. The world does not fight fair, and the only way to fight back is with God on your side. Pushing through on your own will cause you to fall under the pressures of this world.

Who you are can only come to the surface when you are under pressure to be the son or daughter God called you to be. If you hide under false pretenses, you risk suppression of your authentic nature and are not easily distinguishable among the masses. Precious gems are subject to a rough process, but they endure. Endurance increases value.

Each one of us are precious to God's heart. After endurance through the process, our self-worth increases, and we become even more valuable to the Kingdom of God. We are called to be world changers. This requires work and the manifestation of God's plan. God gives insight on how to operate according to His instructions. Growth on the inside reflects itself in an outward glow.

Are you a diamond in the rough? How is your inward growth reflected as an outward glow?

_____

_____

_____

_____

_____

_____

_____

_____

_____

_____

_____

_____

_____

_____

_____

To give up on God is to give up the best life for you and your family. You and everyone around you deserves a brighter future. Ask God to reveal your purpose as guidance and motivation. Pushing through is bigger than you.

What is your plan for pushing through to the Promise Land?

_____

_____

_____

_____

_____

_____

_____

_____

_____

_____

_____

_____

_____

_____

_____

_____

# Gift of Eternal Life

While the 3G Connection suggest we connect to God in three ways, He always gives more than we do. God is greater than any problem we present to Him. You can grow with grace, but God ultimately decides the grace He extends towards His people. You can glow, but you cannot glow the way God intends, without His glory. The glory of God is always greater than an earthly glow.

If you follow the 3G Connection to Go to God, Grow with Grace, and Glow in Glory, you will be lead to the fourth G, which is the Gift of Eternal Life. The greatest gift you can receive is the gift of salvation into eternal life with our Heavenly Father. It is the ultimate sign that we have done what is required of us. When I get to heaven, I want to hear "Well done my good and faithful servant, you have received the gift of eternal life."

Questions and reflections the Holy Spirit prompted me to pose to readers are intended for introspection. Lead by the Holy Spirit, it is my deepest desire that you explored your innermost thoughts and true heart posture. By doing so, you engage in radical self-confrontation. If you engage in the Word of God and quietly wait to hear His voice, the answers may astound you, but encourage growth as well.

Radical confrontation asks you to clearly define who you are. An honest assessment of where you are, where you want to be, and the gap between the two is necessary. As you reflected throughout the time we shared in this book, my prayer is God propels you to where He desires you to be in His mercy. Begin by leading yourself in the Word of God, and by leading others to His grace for His glory.

# 3G Connection with 4G Connectivity

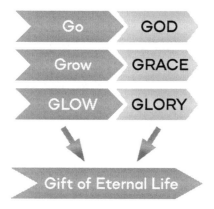

# 3G Biblical References

## Go

"Go therefore and make disciples of all the nations, baptizing them in the name of the Father and of the Son and of the Holy Spirit, teaching them to observe all things that I have commanded you; and lo, I am with you always, even to the end of the age."
**Matthew 28:19-20**

"But seek first the kingdom of God and His righteous-ness, and all these things shall be added to you."
**Matthew 6:33**

"casting all your care upon Him, for He cares for you."
**1 Peter 5:7**

# Grow

"I planted, Apollos watered, but God gave the increase. So then neither be who plants is anything, nor he who waters, but God who gives the increase."
**1 Corinthians 3:6-7**

"for it is sanctified by the word of God and prayer."
**1 Timothy 4:5**

"as newborn babes, desire the pure milk of the word, that you may grow thereby"
**1 Peter 2:2**

# Glow

"But the path of the just is like the shining sun"
**Proverbs 4:18**

"You are the light of the world. A city that is set on a hill cannot be hidden. Nor do they light a lamp and put it under a basket, but on a lampstand, and it gives light to all who are in the house. Let your light so shine before men, that they may see your good works and glorify your Father in heaven."
**Matthews 5: 14-16**

"For I consider that the sufferings of this present time are not worthy to be compared with the glory which shall be revealed in us."
**Romans 8:18**

# God

"God is not a man, that He should lie, Nor a son of man, that He should repent. Has He said, and will He not do? Or has He spoken, and will He not make it good?"

**Numbers 23:19**

"God is Spirit, and those who worship Him must worship Him in spirit and truth."

**John 4:24**

"As for God, His way is perfect; The word of the Lord is proven; He is a shield to all who trust in Him."

**Psalms 18:30**

# Grace

"Again, do you think that we execute ourselves to you? We speak before God in Christ. But we do all things, beloved, for your edification."
**2 Corinthians 12:19**

"For sin shall not have dominion over you, for you are not under law but under grace."
**Romans 6:14**

"Let us therefore come boldly to the throne of grace, that we may obtain mercy and find grace to help in time of need."
**Hebrews 4:16**

# Glory

"But You, O Lord, are a shield for me, My glory and the One who lifts up my head."
**Psalms 3:3**

"For I', says the Lord, 'will be a wall of fire all around her, and I will be the glory in her midst.'"
**Zechariah 2:5**

"Arise, shine; For the glory of the Lord is risen upon you."
**Isaiah 60:1**

# Gift of Eternal Life

"For the wages of sin is death, but the gift of God is
eternal life in Christ Jesus our Lord."
**Romans 6:23**


"keep yourselves in the love of God, looking for the
mercy of our Lord Jesus Christ unto eternal life."
**Jude 1:21**


"Blessed is the man who endures temptation; for
when he has been approved, he will receive the
crown of life which the Lord has promised to those
who love Him."
**James 1:12**

# Natasha Jugger

is available for workshops, speaking engagements,
and as a panel guest.


Connect with the author on social media.

 @3GConnection_

 @3GConnection

 @3GConnection_

 www.blogtalkradio.com/3GConnection

68238550R00100

Made in the USA
Columbia, SC
05 August 2019